DOOM SCROLLING

For Serious Professionals

Devin Blackwell

Mokshadas Press

May all beings be happy and free.

CONTENTS

CHAPTER 1: INTRODUCTION

So, you've spent countless hours doom scrolling—the compulsive act of endlessly refreshing news feeds, absorbing catastrophe after catastrophe, until you're left in a swirling vortex of anxiety, despair, and snack crumbs. Maybe you started as a casual browser, checking headlines here and there. But now, look at you—practically a full-time disaster analyst, glued to your screen, tracking every apocalypse in real-time. Congratulations! You're already halfway to becoming a professional doom scroller.

That's right. The time has come to stop pretending you're just a passive observer of the world's chaos and embrace your true calling. The world of doom scrolling isn't just a hobby—it's a career. And like any good career, it demands dedication, skill development, and, of course, a guidebook to help you master it. That's where this book comes in. Consider it your manual for taking doom scrolling to the next level, where refreshing your newsfeed becomes not just an obsession but a *purpose*.

Why Doom Scrolling? Why Now?

In a world where headlines scream "end of days" every other hour, doom scrolling has become an art form. There's something strangely captivating about staying plugged into the endless stream of bad news—tracking global disasters, decoding cryptic headlines, and predicting which catastrophe will drop next. But it's not enough to just *scroll*; you need to do it with *intention*. That's what separates the professionals from the amateurs.

This book isn't just about how to doom scroll better; it's about turning that relentless anxiety spiral into something productive, or at least something you can laugh about. Think of it as a self-help book for those who thrive in crisis mode—or just love staring into the abyss.

Who This Book Is For

This book is for anyone who has ever spent hours doom scrolling through Twitter, Reddit, news apps, or conspiracy theory websites and thought, *I could be great at this if I just applied myself*. Maybe you've even caught yourself thinking, *There has to be a way to make this my full-time job*. Well, this is your call to action. Whether you're an aspiring doom scroller or a seasoned professional looking to refine your craft, this book is for you.

It's for the perfectionist who wants to maximize their anxiety intake with optimal efficiency. It's for the procrastinator who has turned doom scrolling into an art form of avoiding real responsibilities. And it's for anyone who, despite the world burning around them, still wants to doom scroll in style.

What You'll Learn

Inside these pages, we'll cover the ins and outs of professional doom scrolling, from mastering the perfect scroll station to crafting your own custom doom playlist. You'll learn how to:

- **Set up the ultimate doom scrolling environment**: Comfort, lighting, snacks—everything you need to doom scroll like a pro.

- **Identify and dissect the different types of doom headlines**: From "The World Is Ending" to "Scientists Are Baffled Again," you'll learn to spot the doom traps designed to hook you.

- **Navigate the treacherous jungle of comment sections**: Because what's doom scrolling without engaging with some of the internet's finest keyboard warriors and conspiracy theorists?

- **Laugh at the absurdity of it all**: At some point, you realize that the world is so chaotic it becomes hilarious. This book will teach you how to find humor in the constant barrage of bad news.

- **Balance your doom scrolling with actual life**: Because let's face it, even the most serious professional doom scrollers need to unplug every once in a while (or at least pretend to).

The Future of Doom Scrolling

As we dive deeper into the age of information overload, the world of doom scrolling is evolving. We'll explore the future of this *serious profession*, from AI-driven doom bots to virtual reality doom scrolling, where you can experience the apocalypse from the comfort of your living room. And, if you reach the highest levels of mastery, you might even get recruited into the ranks of **elite doom scrollers**, working for shadowy organizations that monitor global catastrophes in real time (yes, this is a thing, and yes, you want to be a part of it).

Ready to Begin?

If you're ready to embrace your new career as a professional doom scroller, then you've come to the right place. Whether you're in it for the panic, the memes, or the strangely comforting feeling of knowing exactly how doomed we all are, this book will guide you through every step of the process.

So grab your device, get comfortable, and let's start scrolling.

Welcome to the world of professional doom scrolling —where every catastrophe is an opportunity, and every refresh brings you closer to mastering your craft.

CHAPTER 2: THE ART OF SCROLLING

Every great craft requires dedication, technique, and, of course, that perfect balance between genius and complete chaos. Welcome, doom scroller, to the elite ranks of those who have mastered the delicate dance of doom. You might think all you need is a phone and a general disdain for good news—but, oh no. There's more to it than that.

Doom scrolling is a **skill**. It's not just about aimlessly thumbing through disaster after disaster—it's about cultivating an intentional rhythm of despair and discovery, all while staring blankly at your screen for hours at a time. You're not just someone who "scrolls"—you're a digital warrior, standing tall (or more likely, slumped over) at the edge of the apocalypse.

Types of Doom Scrollers

Let's start by identifying what kind of doom scroller you are. Self-awareness is key in this journey, and not all doom scrollers are created equal. There are several distinct species of doom scrollers. Which one are you?

1. The Night Owl

You're a late-night lurker, scrolling through the endless sea of despair while the world sleeps. Whether it's insomnia, a busy schedule, or just the fact that the darkest thoughts come alive at 3 a.m., you are a master of nocturnal doom consumption. By the time the sun rises, you've not only absorbed every global crisis but can also name the top 10 Twitter meltdowns of the past 12 hours.

Your strength: Insatiable curiosity and the ability to remain awake while everyone else is blissfully unconscious. Your weakness: Absolutely no one to talk to about your findings at 4 a.m., except other doom scroll addicts… or your cat.

2. The Morning Dreader

You wake up, groggily grab your phone, and immediately plunge into despair. Before your coffee is even brewed, you've already seen five news stories about the inevitable collapse of civilization. You're the kind of person who doesn't believe in starting the day without a strong jolt of panic.

Your strength: Efficiency. You can doom scroll before breakfast. You multitask like a pro, managing existential dread and toast-making simultaneously. Your weakness: That overwhelming sense of dread you feel by 9 a.m., and your blood pressure probably isn't thrilled either.

3. The Midday Masochist

You get a few hours of peace in the morning, maybe even accomplish some actual work, but by noon, it's time for a little despair snack. You've barely finished your lunch before you're scrolling through the latest catastrophe—whether it's geopolitical upheaval or someone's 700-tweet thread about the economy collapsing.

Your strength: Strategic scrolling. You pace yourself like a pro, only taking in small servings of doom throughout the day. Your weakness: You're unable to enjoy a sandwich without wondering if it's your last lunch before societal breakdown.

4. The Weekend Warrior

All week long, you tell yourself you'll wait. You'll live in ignorant bliss for a few days, handle your life like a responsible adult. Then the weekend hits, and like a dam bursting, you are in it. Your phone screen gets more attention than your partner, friends, or even that expensive brunch you planned. By Sunday night, you've consumed so much doom you're practically a walking Wikipedia of impending disasters.

Your strength: You've somehow convinced yourself you're "taking a break" during the week, which makes you feel better about your weekend benders. Your weakness: Monday morning existential hangovers. You start the workweek with the energy of a used dishrag.

The Perfect Scroll Setup

Now that you've figured out what kind of doom scroller you are, let's get into the essentials. The art of scrolling isn't just about what you read—it's about how you set the mood. You wouldn't drink wine out of a paper cup, would you? So why would you doom scroll without the proper setup?

1. Lighting

You need dim lighting. It creates the perfect atmosphere of vague hopelessness without completely wrecking your eyesight. Think "gloomy cave" meets "I haven't left my room in 24 hours." If your phone brightness is set to "blinding," you're doing it wrong. Adjust accordingly.

2. Posture

The professional doom scroller has several ideal postures, including:

- **The Hunch:** Classic. Ideal for mid-spiral, when you're too engrossed in a debate about global warming to sit up straight.

- **The Bed Slump:** Best for nighttime scrolling. Make sure you're half-buried in blankets, because nothing screams "I'm handling this well" like looking like a caterpillar in a cocoon.

- **The Couch Potato:** A good all-day option. Legs up, phone in hand, and a growing pile of snacks next to you. Ignore the crumbs. You'll clean them up once you finish this next doom spiral… or the next one after that.

3. Snacks

A true doom scrolling session is not complete without sustenance. Consider these:

- **Chips:** They're crunchy, salty, and provide a satisfying distraction from your existential dread.

- **Popcorn:** Perfect for scrolling through political debates—it adds the feeling that you're watching a slow-motion disaster movie.

- **Chocolate:** For when you need a pick-me-up, because nothing combats the inevitable heat death of the universe like sugar.

Exercises for Building Scroll Stamina

Scrolling through bad news for hours on end isn't easy. You need to build your endurance like an athlete in training—except your training involves not throwing your phone across the room every time you read a headline.

1. Start Small

Begin with local disasters, like traffic updates or small-town controversies ("Mayor accused of stealing Halloween candy—Details at 11"). These aren't life-ruining, but they'll get your brain into the groove of outrage.

2. Take Doom Breaks

After 45 minutes of scrolling, your brain might try to rebel. Don't let it. Give yourself a 5-minute breather—look at cute animal photos or videos of babies laughing. You need to keep your soul slightly intact for the long haul.

3. Return Stronger

Once you've worked your way up to the big leagues (climate change, financial collapse, existential crises about AI taking over the world), take pride in your progress. You've leveled up, my friend. You are now capable of absorbing the world's chaos *and* functioning as a human being. Kind of.

Final Thoughts

Doom scrolling is a marathon, not a sprint. It's an art, a practice, a lifestyle. Remember, it's all about balance. You're not here to win, because there is no winning when the news is constantly terrible. Instead, you're here to participate, to scroll with the best of them, and to craft your own little corner of despair.

Up next, we'll talk about Headlines from the Void—where you'll learn why every piece of news seems like the end of the world, and how to spot the most outrageous, clickbait-worthy stories like a true pro.

CHAPTER 3: HEADLINES FROM THE VOID

Have you ever noticed that every headline these days reads like a dramatic movie trailer? There's no "neutral" news anymore. It's all extremes. Every article is either about the imminent end of civilization or the discovery of a new avocado toast recipe that's somehow going to change your life forever. Welcome to the world of modern journalism—a place where even the mildest occurrence can be inflated to apocalyptic proportions.

Doom scrolling thrives in this environment. These headlines aren't just informative, they're engineered to *hook* you, to pull you in, and to make you think, *"Wait, what now? The polar ice caps are melting faster than ice cream on a hot sidewalk?!"* And before you know it, you've clicked through 17 articles, each more anxiety-inducing than the last.

But not all headlines are created equal. In this chapter, we'll explore the different types of "doom-worthy" headlines and learn to distinguish between a mild inconvenience and full-blown chaos. Because let's be real—sometimes it's hard to tell the difference.

The 'End of the World' Headline

This is the doom scroller's bread and butter. Any headline that makes you feel like the world is teetering on the edge of the abyss is sure to get clicks —and keep you scrolling through hours of articles about how doomed we are.

Examples:

- "Climate Change Reaches Point of No Return: Experts Say We Have 5 Minutes Left to Act"

- "Asteroid on Collision Course with Earth? NASA Scientists Are Concerned"

- "Supervolcano Eruption Could Wipe Out Humanity Next Tuesday, But Scientists Are Still Baffled"

These headlines are crafted to inspire both awe and terror. They usually start with a powerful phrase like "point of no return" or "scientists baffled," which is code for "you should probably be panicking right now." If you see one of these, congratulations! You've hit the doom scrolling jackpot.

How to Respond:

- Click immediately. Then click related articles. Then look up NASA's website for further confirmation. Is humanity truly on the brink? You need to know!

The 'Baffled Scientists' Headline

Scientists are always baffled. Have you noticed? They're baffled by mysterious space signals, baffled by strange diseases, baffled by the extinction of bees. Every time something baffling happens, you're required by doom scrolling law to investigate.

Examples:

- "Mysterious Space Object Baffles Scientists— Could It Be Alien Technology?"

- "New, Highly Contagious Disease Baffles Doctors—What You Need to Know"

- "Scientists Baffled as Swarms of Murder Hornets

Invade New York"

Nothing quite gets the doom scroll juices flowing like a headline about confused scientists. If they, the supposed experts, don't know what's going on, how are we supposed to make sense of it? It's the perfect recipe for anxiety.

How to Respond:

- Set aside at least 30 minutes to fall into a rabbit hole of baffling scientific mysteries. Bonus points if you end up on a conspiracy theory forum.

The 'You're Probably Dying' Headline

This one's a personal favorite for the hypochondriacs among us. It's the headline that takes a common, everyday occurrence and turns it into something that makes you question whether you're on the verge of spontaneous combustion.

Examples:

- "New Study Shows Sitting for More Than 2 Hours Could Shorten Your Life by 12 Years"

- "Experts Warn: Your Phone Might Be Slowly Poisoning You—Here's Why"

- "Is Your Morning Coffee Killing You? What New

Research Reveals"

In the world of doom scrolling, everything is dangerous. Every food, every drink, every piece of furniture in your house is potentially fatal. It's like the Grim Reaper is just sitting there, watching you live your life, waiting for that one cup of coffee to push you over the edge.

How to Respond:

- Panic. Google all symptoms, conditions, and new research to ensure you're not unknowingly bringing about your own demise. Then drink a green juice just in case.

The 'Financial Collapse Is Nigh' Headline

This one hits a little too close to home. It's the headline that makes you rethink every financial decision you've ever made—from investing in crypto to spending $5 on a fancy latte.

Examples:

- "Global Recession Imminent: Here's How to Protect Your Finances"

- "Stock Market Crashes: What This Means for Your Retirement"

- "Economists Warn: The Dollar Could Collapse by Year's End"

The world of finance is a scary place, especially when headlines make it sound like we're always on the brink of total economic collapse. These headlines prey on your deepest financial insecurities, ensuring you spend at least two hours rethinking your entire savings strategy. Spoiler alert: You don't have one, because you're too busy doom scrolling.

How to Respond:

- Read 10 articles about the impending financial apocalypse, then check your bank account and cry softly into your pillow.

The 'Celebrity Meltdown' Headline

While not exactly "doom" in the traditional sense, the celebrity meltdown headline is the perfect break from global catastrophe. These headlines allow you to indulge in someone else's chaos for a bit, giving you a brief respite from your own existential despair.

Examples:

- "Celebrity X's Twitter Rant: Are They Losing Their Mind?"

- "Reality TV Star Arrested After Bizarre Public

Outburst"

- "Famous Actor Leaves Hollywood Amid Wild Conspiracy Theories"

There's nothing quite like a good celebrity meltdown to distract you from your worries. It's like a mini-vacation from the end of the world. Sure, society may be crumbling, but at least you're not the one getting into public feuds with strangers on Twitter.

How to Respond:

- Enjoy the drama. Maybe scroll through the celeb's social media for extra fun. Then return to the apocalypse at hand.

The 'Everything is Breaking' Headline

We live in a world where everything is apparently malfunctioning at all times—airlines, the internet, the power grid. These headlines make you feel like every system that keeps society running is perpetually on the verge of collapse. It's like Murphy's Law for the modern world: If it can break, it will.

Examples:

- "Air Traffic Control Systems Fail Across the Globe: What Happens Now?"

- "Internet Outages Plague Major Cities—Is This the New Normal?"

- "Power Grid Failing? Experts Warn of Blackouts During Summer Heatwaves"

These headlines are designed to keep you on edge. What if the internet goes out *right now*? What if the power grid collapses during your doom scrolling session? It's chaos, and you need to stay informed.

How to Respond:

- Panic-scroll while you still have electricity and Wi-Fi. Stock up on candles, bottled water, and maybe some extra phone chargers—just in case.

The 'Completely Random and Terrifying' Headline

Then, there are the oddball headlines. The ones that don't seem to fit into any specific category but are terrifying nonetheless. These articles present bizarre events that make you question reality itself.

Examples:

- "Invasion of Giant Flying Spiders Reported in Several States"

- "Mysterious Sounds from Deep Space Continue

to Puzzle Astronomers"

- "Scientists Confirm Earth's Magnetic Poles Are Shifting Faster Than Expected—What Does This Mean?"

These are the headlines that trigger the, "Well, I didn't see THAT coming" reaction. They're random, weird, and just unsettling enough to make you think the universe is actively trying to mess with you.

How to Respond:

Prepare for giant spiders, shifting magnetic poles, and alien invasions. Maybe build a bunker. And don't forget to doom scroll from inside it.

Why Headlines Hook You

You might wonder why these headlines are so addictive. Well, they're designed to be. Journalists and content creators know how to tap into our brains' deepest fears and anxieties. There's an actual science behind the way headlines are crafted, meant to keep you reading, clicking, and—most importantly—*scrolling*.

It's not just about informing you—it's about keeping you on edge. And let's be honest: we doom scrollers love being on edge. We thrive on it. We want to feel like we're living in a constant state of suspense, where the next headline could be the one that finally pushes us over.

Your Daily Headline Checklist

By now, you should be able to spot the different types of doom headlines with ease. As you move forward in your doom scrolling journey, remember to diversify your headline intake. You want a balanced diet of existential terror, financial collapse, baffled scientists, and, of course, celebrity meltdowns.

Up next, we'll dive into the comment section jungle, where we'll explore the wild, untamed chaos that lurks beneath every article. Spoiler alert: It's even worse than the headlines.

CHAPTER 4:
THE COMMENT
SECTION JUNGLE

Congratulations! You've made it past the headlines—now, welcome to the digital Wild West, where logic goes to die, opinions are wielded like weapons, and everyone is a self-proclaimed expert. That's right, we're talking about the comment section.

For some, the comment section is a place to engage in meaningful dialogue, exchange ideas, and perhaps even learn something new. But for the doom scroller? Oh, no. The comment section is your next level of *doom immersion*, a twisted playground where chaos reigns and where you can watch humanity unravel in real-time. It's like nature documentaries, but instead of animals, it's humans losing their minds over anything from pineapple on pizza to geopolitics.

In this chapter, we'll guide you through the treacherous terrain of online comments, identifying the types of commenters you'll encounter and providing strategies for navigating the madness. Grab your helmet—you're going to need it.

The Keyboard Warrior

Ah, the mighty Keyboard Warrior—a fearless fighter of the virtual battlefield. This person has strong opinions on literally everything, and they will defend those opinions with the ferocity of a cornered honey badger. They see the comment section as their personal battleground, a place to conquer dissenters with sheer force of CAPS LOCK and endless walls of text.

Characteristics:

- Replies to everyone, even when no one asked.

- Uses ALL CAPS when they want to make an especially important point, which is usually every 15 seconds.

- Never concedes defeat. Ever. Even when proven wrong, they will circle back with, "But actually…"

How to Spot Them:

Look for the comment thread that's at least 47 replies deep, where the original post was something innocuous like, "Does anyone know a good pizza place around here?" The Keyboard Warrior has somehow turned it into a full-blown debate on politics, climate change, or why their pizza opinions are the only correct ones.

How to Respond:

> Don't engage. Seriously, walk away. The Warrior thrives on combat, and by the time you've replied, they've already written a 10,000-word essay on why pineapple doesn't belong on pizza, complete with citations.

The Conspiracy Theorist

This person knows something the rest of us don't—or so they claim. To them, everything is connected, and *nothing* is as it seems. The moon landing? Fake. Vaccines? Government mind control. The weather? Controlled by the Illuminati. They'll drop into a comment section like a ninja, casually mentioning that whatever you're discussing is part of a larger, sinister plot orchestrated by secret global powers.

Characteristics:

- Always brings up "hidden truths" or "what the

mainstream media won't tell you."

- Links to sketchy YouTube videos that look like they were filmed in someone's basement.

- Phrases like "Wake up, sheeple!" and "Do your own research!" are their battle cry.

How to Spot Them:

They'll hijack any conversation, no matter how irrelevant. A simple article about endangered turtles? Conspiracy Theorist: "Turtles are dying because the government's secretly testing 5G in the oceans to control the weather. WAKE UP."

How to Respond:

Nod, smile, and slowly back away. There's no winning here. You could try to debunk their theories, but this will only fuel their belief that *you* are part of the cover-up.

The Grammar Cop

The Grammar Cop cares about one thing, and one thing only—proper grammar. Forget the content of your comment—did you just use "their" when you meant "they're"? Oh boy, it's on now. This person lives to correct other people's spelling and grammar, and they don't care how irrelevant it is to the conversation at hand.

Characteristics:

- Doesn't contribute anything meaningful to the discussion, but will point out every misplaced apostrophe like it's a capital offense.

- Feels morally superior because they know the difference between "affect" and "effect."

- Will derail a thread about global warming to discuss the Oxford comma.

How to Spot Them:

You've just posted an insightful comment about how we can address climate change, and instead of engaging with your ideas, the Grammar Cop swoops in with, "*Actually*, you used 'there' instead of 'their,' so your argument is invalid." Thanks, buddy. That's helpful.

How to Respond:

Resist the urge to reply with a typo on purpose. You're better than that... aren't you?

The "Well, Actually" Guy

You could say the sky is blue, and this person would show up to say, "Well, actually, it's more of a cerulean hue based on the diffraction of light waves through the atmosphere." They're here to correct you, to let you know that whatever you just said, they know better. It's their way of life.

Characteristics:

- Phrases every response with, "Well, actually..." before launching into an unnecessary correction.

- Never offers new information—just nitpicks minor details to show they're smarter.

- Makes every conversation feel like a lecture, except nobody asked them to teach anything.

How to Spot Them:

No matter how basic or factual your statement is, "Well, Actually" Guy has a slight correction. You: "It's raining pretty hard today." Them: "Well, actually, this is technically considered a 'light drizzle' according to meteorological standards."

How to Respond:

- **Play dumb**: Respond with, "Wow, I didn't know that, thank you!" This confuses them because they thrive on confrontation. Without resistance, they'll slowly vanish like a fart in the wind.

The Meme Lord

The Meme Lord is here for one thing and one thing only: chaos through humor. Their role in the comment section is to drop memes and GIFs that range from hilariously on-point to completely irrelevant. No matter the topic, they have a meme for it.

Characteristics:

- Speaks almost entirely in memes and reaction GIFs.

- Treats every conversation as an opportunity to troll—*but in a fun way.*

- Gets a weird amount of upvotes despite adding absolutely no substance to the conversation.

How to Spot Them:

You're in the middle of a serious discussion about climate change, and suddenly there's a GIF of Kermit the Frog sipping tea, followed by a meme about how 2020 was the longest decade of their life. Somehow, it's the highest-rated comment on the thread.

How to Respond:

Join in the fun. Drop a meme in return and bask

in the pointless hilarity. The Meme Lord thrives on random chaos, and sometimes, that's the break you need in your doom scrolling journey.

The Concern Troll

The Concern Troll seems polite and well-meaning at first, but don't be fooled—they're here to subtly undermine you. They'll drop comments like, "I'm just worried that you're not thinking this through," or "I'm really concerned that you're spreading misinformation," all while pretending to be the reasonable one. In reality, they're there to stir the pot without getting their hands dirty.

Characteristics:

- Passive-aggressive tone masked as politeness.

- Ends every comment with "I'm just concerned for your well-being."

- Manages to derail conversations with subtle but pointed jabs.

How to Spot Them:

You've just shared an opinion, and here comes the Concern Troll: "I see where you're coming from, but I'm concerned that you haven't done enough research on this topic. Have you considered you might be dangerously misinformed?"

How to Respond:

- **Be overly nice**: "Wow, thank you so much for your concern! I'll be sure to recheck everything I've ever thought about in life." It'll drive them nuts.

The Ghost

The Ghost is a mysterious commenter who shows up, drops a wildly controversial opinion, and then disappears into the digital ether. No replies, no explanations—just a single comment left to wreak havoc on the discussion.

Characteristics:

- One and done. They never return to defend their hot take.

- Their comments are often deliberately provocative, ensuring maximum chaos.

- Everyone wonders: who are they? Where did they go? Are they watching the carnage unfold from the shadows?

How to Spot Them:

You'll know the Ghost by the aftermath—after their

comment, the thread erupts into chaos, but they are nowhere to be found. They've vanished, leaving behind only a trail of confusion and rage.

How to Respond:

Don't bother. They're gone. Off to ruin another thread. All you can do is marvel at their mysterious power.

Surviving the Jungle

The comment section is a lawless place, a digital jungle where survival is not guaranteed. But now, with this guide, you are prepared. You know the species of commenters you'll encounter, and you can navigate the chaos like a pro.

Remember, the golden rule of the comment section is: don't feed the trolls. And if all else fails, there's always the classic escape—close the browser, throw your phone across the room, and go take a walk. Just kidding. You're a doom scroller. You'll be back.

In the next chapter, we'll tackle Social Media: Doom, But Make It Pretty, where we'll explore the twisted beauty of Instagram, Twitter wars, and how everyone's living a seemingly perfect life while you're still in bed doom scrolling.

CHAPTER 5:
SOCIAL MEDIA:
DOOM, BUT MAKE
IT PRETTY

In the grand hierarchy of doom scrolling, social media is the crown jewel, the gleaming beacon of beautifully packaged chaos. It's where the collapse of civilization meets pastel filters, where world events are summarized in 280 characters, and where your high school acquaintance somehow manages to own a yacht despite never finishing a single group project. In short, it's the most addictive and soul-crushing corner of the internet.

Social media is where doom scrolling thrives, because unlike news websites, social media *feels* personal. This isn't just faceless news—these are people you know (and sometimes wish you didn't), people who have hot takes, moral outrage, and the inexplicable urge to share their every waking thought about the world falling apart.

In this chapter, we'll break down the different platforms, the unique flavor of doom each one serves, and why you're inexplicably drawn to watching it all unfold—while questioning every life choice you've ever made.

Instagram: Doom, But Make It Aesthetic

Ah, Instagram—the land of filtered sunsets, artfully arranged brunches, and motivational quotes that somehow make you feel worse about yourself. It's not just about pretty pictures; it's about the *curation* of life, the delicate balance of showing off your best self while pretending you're not trying too hard.

But Instagram has a darker side, especially for the doom scroller. It's where you see the world's problems filtered through a haze of soft lighting and hashtags. If you want to see someone announce the end of the world while wearing a cute summer dress, Instagram's your place.

How Instagram Feeds Your Doom Habit:

- **Perfect Lives:** Your friends are all having the best time of their lives while you're still trying to figure out how to reheat leftovers. Someone's in Bali, someone else is drinking an acai smoothie in a cafe that looks like it was designed by angels. Meanwhile, your biggest accomplishment of the day was remembering to brush your teeth.

- **Activist Influencers:** Nothing says "I'm deeply concerned about climate change" like posting a selfie with a reusable straw. Instagram activists know how to package doom as part of their brand. Expect posts like, "Saving the world, one avocado toast at a time. #blessed #savetheplanet #influencerlife."

- **Doomscroll & Shop:** Instagram cleverly combines world-ending anxiety with consumerism. "The world might be ending, but you can still look great doing it! Click the link in my bio to shop my apocalypse wardrobe."

How to Survive:

- Embrace the absurdity. Every time you see someone living their best life, remind yourself that behind that perfectly filtered photo is probably a half-eaten bowl of cereal and existential dread.

- Follow accounts that share ridiculous memes about the end of the world—it'll make the doom scroll much more entertaining. Nothing softens the blow of environmental catastrophe quite like a perfectly timed cat meme.

X / Twitter: The Hellscape of Hot Takes

If Instagram is the soft glow of doom, Twitter (now "X") is the fire hose of outrage, blasting 280-character opinions at you from all directions. X is where you go if you want to feel personally attacked by strangers for saying something as simple as, "Pineapple on pizza is fine." It's the digital equivalent of walking into a room and everyone immediately starts yelling.

But for doom scrollers, X is now the ultimate fix. Real-time news, debates, meltdowns, and celebrity feuds—all condensed into bite-sized pieces that keep you hitting "refresh" like it's your job.

How X Feeds Your Doom Habit:

- **Outrage Culture:** Every day on Twitter, someone new is being "canceled." You don't even need to know who they are—just watching the digital pitchforks come out is enough to fuel your doom scrolling for hours.

- **Trending Topics of Terror:** Twitter knows exactly how to trigger your anxiety by putting global disasters front and center. You open the app, and BOOM—there's a hashtag trending about the latest wildfire, stock market crash, or alien invasion (because, honestly, at this point, why not?).

- **Moral Panics:** Twitter's moral panic cycles are legendary. One day, the world's ending because of climate change, the next, we're all doomed because someone wore the wrong Halloween costume. Either way, it's a buffet of outrage for you to feast on.

How to Survive:

- Limit your exposure to the outrage. Pick a few accounts to follow that make you laugh, share interesting information, or post absurd tweets that have nothing to do with the world falling apart.

- Make use of the mute and block buttons like you're Neo dodging bullets in *The Matrix*. You don't need to see every hot take—just the ones that make you feel slightly less doomed.

- Try creating a Twitter list titled "Good

Vibes Only" and fill it with puppies, wholesome memes, and inspirational quotes. (You'll never use it, but it's nice to know it's there.)

Facebook: Where Doom and Aunt Linda's Memes Collide

Facebook is the Swiss Army knife of doom scrolling. It's got everything: global disasters, conspiracy theories, high school reunion updates, and, of course, Aunt Linda sharing a 12-paragraph rant about how the government is secretly turning squirrels into spies.

The doom scroller's journey on Facebook is one of unpredictability. One minute, you're looking at photos of your cousin's wedding, and the next, you're knee-deep in a thread about why the moon landing was fake.

How Facebook Feeds Your Doom Habit:

- **Political Rants:** Facebook is the place where people you haven't spoken to in 10 years suddenly become experts on geopolitics. Nothing says "I care about the fate of the world" like a furious post about how traffic lights are actually symbols of government oppression.

- **Conspiracy Central:** If there's one thing Facebook is great at, it's spreading misinformation. You'll find threads where people debate everything from 5G towers to flat Earth theories, all while aggressively tagging their friends.

- **Doomscrolling With a Side of Nostalgia:** Facebook likes to remind you of "memories" from years ago, making sure you're aware that not only is the world worse now, but also that you peaked in 2012.

How to Survive:

- Engage only with the funniest, most unhinged conspiracy theories. You'll be amazed by the creativity. "Did you know the government controls the weather via invisible lizards? Neither did I, but thanks to Facebook, I'm now terrified!"

- Hide posts from overly dramatic relatives. Aunt Linda can continue her crusade against chemtrails without your input.

- Join groups that celebrate absurd humor—like "Cats Who Are Doing Important Things"—to offset the gloom.

TikTok: The End of the World,

but Make It Dance

TikTok, the rising star of social media, is a fast-paced, chaotic paradise for doom scrollers with short attention spans. Here, you can watch teenagers dance to the latest viral song, and then—boom—a video about climate collapse. The beauty of TikTok is that it whips you from joy to despair in the span of a 15-second video, which is *perfect* for doom scrolling.

How TikTok Feeds Your Doom Habit:

- **Whiplash Content:** TikTok gives you emotional whiplash. One second, you're watching someone dance in a shark costume, the next, you're watching a video about how rising sea levels are going to drown entire cities. It's the digital equivalent of switching between a rom-com and a disaster movie every few seconds.

- **Gen Z Prophecies:** Gen Z is both the most existentially aware generation and the most likely to turn their existential despair into content. TikTok is full of teenagers who joke about the apocalypse like it's a given, which, honestly, is both comforting and terrifying.

- **ConspiracyTok:** Oh, you thought Facebook had a monopoly on conspiracy theories? Welcome to TikTok, where you can fall down a rabbit hole of wild theories about aliens, shadow governments, and time travel—all narrated over a catchy beat.

How to Survive:

- **Set a Time Limit:** TikTok's addictive algorithm will keep feeding you content until you forget what daylight looks like. Consider setting an alarm—or else you'll look up and realize three hours have passed, and you've learned absolutely nothing useful.

- **Curate Your Feed**: If you're getting too much doom and not enough dance videos, start liking every video of baby animals you can find. TikTok's algorithm will adjust, and soon you'll be watching puppies instead of apocalyptic forecasts.

- **Accept Tthe Chaos:** TikTok is like the digital version of throwing confetti in the air and seeing where it lands. Sometimes it's fun, sometimes it's a disaster, but either way, you'll be entertained.

Doom Scroll With Style

Each social media platform offers its own unique flavor of doom, packaged with just the right amount of distractions to keep you hooked. Instagram presents doom with an aesthetic, Twitter with rage, Facebook with a side of conspiracy, and TikTok with dance challenges and existential humor. It's a beautiful mess, and you're right in the middle of it.

Next time you're on social media, remember: it's all a performance. Behind every perfectly crafted post or snarky tweet is someone just as confused and doomed as you. So scroll on, my friend. But maybe throw in a cat video or two for balance.

In the next chapter, we'll dive into the Doom Scroller's Social Guide, where we'll discuss how to navigate real-life conversations when someone brings up the fact that you've been reading the news at 3 a.m. while everyone else is sleeping soundly.

CHAPTER 6: THE DOOM SCROLLER'S SOCIAL GUIDE

So, you've spent hours (or days... who's counting?) scrolling through endless waves of global calamities, political meltdowns, and celebrity breakups. You're now thoroughly marinated in despair, well-versed in all the ways the world might end, and you've cultivated an impressive bank of useless but terrifying knowledge. Now comes the hard part: talking to actual people about your newfound expertise in doom.

Whether it's at a dinner party, a work meeting, or an awkward elevator ride, people are bound to bring up current events. And who better than you, the doom scrolling pro, to drop some soul-crushing facts about the state of the world? But here's the tricky part— while you might be deep in the doom spiral, other people are still trying to *function* in society without being reminded that we're all doomed. So how do you contribute without sucking all the air out of the room?

This chapter is your guide to navigating these treacherous waters. You'll learn how to talk about the world's disasters without turning every social interaction into a therapy session or scaring off your friends. Let's get started.

Don't Be "That Person" at the Party

We all know *that* person. They're the one who, halfway through a perfectly lovely conversation about someone's vacation, casually drops, "You know, the Great Barrier Reef is dying, right?" Instantly, the mood shifts from lighthearted banter to deep, existential dread. While you may feel compelled to share the doom (it's important to be informed, right?), remember: timing is everything.

How to Avoid Doom-Bombing:

- **Gauge the room:** If everyone's talking about TV shows, pet antics, or vacation plans, it's probably not the time to bring up climate change. Save your heavy facts for when the conversation shifts to more serious topics.

- **Blend in, don't dominate:** Nobody wants to be cornered by the person who turns every conversation into a TED Talk about the state of the planet. It's okay to chime in, but let others guide the conversation too.

- **Use humor:** If you must bring up something dark, soften the blow with humor. "Yeah, the polar ice caps are melting… but hey, at least we'll all have beachfront property soon, right?"

The Art of the Casual Fact Drop

When you've been doom scrolling, you accumulate a *lot* of information that others may not have come across yet. But rather than overwhelming people with grim statistics, the key is to sprinkle your knowledge into conversations without hijacking them. Think of it like seasoning a dish—you want just enough to add flavor, but not so much that it becomes inedible.

Examples of a Good Fact Drop:

- **At a BBQ:** "This grilled chicken is amazing! Did

you know that rising temperatures are affecting poultry farming? It's fascinating how climate change impacts our food supply."

- **At the gym:** "I love this workout. Oh, by the way, have you seen the latest studies on how sitting for more than eight hours a day is slowly killing us?"

- **On a walk with friends:** "What a gorgeous sunset. It's a shame pollution's contributing to those stunning colors—apparently, particulate matter in the air does that. Who knew?"

You see? Light, casual, and mildly terrifying, but not overwhelming. The goal is to educate, not cause panic attacks.

How to Handle the Blank Stares

Not everyone has the same level of doom-awareness as you, and that's okay. But occasionally, you'll hit people with a perfectly valid doom nugget only to be met with blank stares. This is not a sign to double down and explain in even greater detail why sea levels are rising. Instead, it's time to pivot and *gently* change the subject before people start mentally checking out.

How to Recover:

- **Use a diversion:** "Yeah, it's wild how much the world is changing... anyway, have you tried the nachos yet? They're incredible!"

- **Blame the algorithm:** "I know, I sound like a broken record. I swear, the algorithm just keeps feeding me this stuff! Maybe I need to follow more dog accounts."

- **Play it off:** "Don't mind me, I've been reading too much news lately. Let's talk about something less depressing—like your vacation plans!"

Remember, you're not trying to bum everyone out; you're just *really* well-informed. It's all about knowing when to retreat.

The Social Media Quandary

At some point, someone's going to ask, "Where do you get all your news from?" Be prepared. If you admit to getting most of your information from Twitter, Reddit, or Facebook, they might look at you like you just admitted to consulting a magic 8-ball for life advice. The trick is to casually mix in some *real* sources with your doom scroll faves. (Nobody needs to know that half of your doom comes from a thread started by someone named "ConspiracyKing420".)

Acceptable Responses:

- "Oh, you know, a little bit of everywhere—BBC, NPR, The New York Times, and sometimes Twitter for real-time updates."

- "I try to stay informed with a mix of major news outlets, but I also follow a few accounts on social media that post quick updates—helps me keep track of what's happening in the world."

- "I like reading longer investigative pieces, but honestly, Twitter keeps me up-to-date on breaking news."

This way, you come off as informed and savvy, not as someone spiraling into the depths of Reddit conspiracy forums at 3 a.m.

Pivoting Away from Doom: A Survival Guide

Sometimes, you'll realize mid-conversation that you've gone too far down the doom rabbit hole. Maybe you started innocently enough with a comment about the economy, but suddenly you're discussing population decline, collapsing ecosystems, and robots taking over all jobs by 2030. The room is silent. Everyone's staring at you like you just predicted the apocalypse (which, let's face it, you kind of did).

When this happens, it's time to pivot. Shift the conversation back to something lighter—*anything* lighter.

Phrases to Help You Pivot:

- "But who knows, right? Let's just enjoy today!"

- "Enough about that—tell me, what's the latest on that Netflix show everyone's talking about?"

- "It's crazy to think about, but hey, at least we don't have to worry about that today. What's everyone doing this weekend?"

By pivoting, you show that you're capable of *not* dooming the entire room, and you can return to being a normal person for the remainder of the social event. (Until you get home and start doom scrolling again, of course.)

Fun Small Talk Starters for

the Doom-Immune

Some people just aren't ready for the truth, and that's okay. They live in a blissful bubble of optimism and ignorance. When you find yourself in a situation where doom scrolling isn't an appropriate topic (think baby showers, first dates, and casual chit-chat at the grocery store), here are some safer conversation starters that *won't* remind people of impending disaster:

- "Have you seen any good movies lately?"

- "What's your favorite comfort food?"

- "If you could travel anywhere in the world right now, where would it be?"

- "What's the most ridiculous thing you've seen on TV lately?"

These topics are safe, fun, and unlikely to spiral into existential panic. Keep them in your back pocket for when doom scrolling chatter is off-limits, and your social skills will be *chef's kiss*.

Navigating the Apocalypse Together: Group Therapy for Doom Scrollers

Occasionally, you'll meet another doom scroller. This is the unicorn of social interactions—a fellow traveler who also spends their nights deep in Reddit threads about how the bees are disappearing and why AI is probably already smarter than us.

When you find someone like this, it's okay to let your guard down and have a *real* conversation about the doom you've both been soaking in. But be careful—this is not a free pass to turn the interaction into a two-person doomsday cult. Keep it light, share a few laughs about how absurdly informed you are, and—most importantly—end on a positive note.

How to Keep It Balanced:

- Share a few doom tidbits, but always balance it out with humor: "Yeah, the polar ice caps are melting at an alarming rate, but hey, at least I won't have to travel as far for a beach vacation, right?"

- Find common ground: "Do you ever find it comforting to know that if the world ends, at least we've been preparing for it mentally for years now?"

- Make sure to laugh: Doom scrolling is dark, but if you can't laugh at it, it'll consume you. Share memes, absurd news stories, and always leave the conversation feeling a little lighter.

The Art of Doom, Lightly

Being a doom scroller doesn't mean you have to doom your social life. With the right approach, you can share your knowledge of the world's impending disasters without ruining every party. Remember, the key is balance. You can't stop scrolling, but you *can* stop yourself from dragging everyone else into the abyss with you.

In the next chapter, we'll get into Doom Scrolling Like a Pro, where we'll share advanced tips and tricks for mastering the art of doom, from setting up your perfect scroll station to crafting the ultimate panic playlist.

CHAPTER 7: DOOM SCROLLING LIKE A PRO

You've been practicing the art of doom scrolling for a while now. You've gotten pretty good at it—maybe even too good. But as with any skill, there's always room for improvement. In this chapter, we'll take your doom scrolling game to the next level. After all, why be a casual doom scroller when you can be a professional?

Mastering the art of doom scrolling isn't just about what you read—it's about how you do it. The tools, the techniques, the mindset. You're not just absorbing bad news; you're creating an entire doom scrolling *experience*. You'll learn how to set up the perfect scroll station, optimize your scrolling technique, and, of course, create the ultimate soundtrack to accompany your descent into the abyss.

Are you ready to elevate your game? Let's get scrolling.

The Perfect Scroll Setup: Building Your Doom Den

If you're going to spend hours plunging into the depths of digital despair, you might as well do it in style. You need a dedicated space where you can lose yourself in the endless waves of bad news without interruption. Think of it as your personal Doom Den —a place where anxiety and snack crumbs come together in perfect harmony.

Essentials for the Ultimate Scroll Station:

- **Dim Lighting:** We covered this briefly before, but let's dive deeper. The lighting in your scroll station should set the mood—dark enough to feel like you're spiraling into the void, but not so dark that you strain your eyes. Aim for something between "early 2000s vampire movie" and "mild existential crisis."

- **Comfortable Seating:** You'll be here for a while, so comfort is key. Whether it's a cozy couch, a bean bag chair, or a pile of blankets that looks suspiciously like a nest, make sure you can settle in for the long haul.

- **Multiple Screens (Optional, but Highly Recommended):** Why doom scroll on one screen when you can use two (or more)? With a dual-monitor setup, you can read a news article on one screen while keeping an eye on Twitter meltdowns on the other. Or maybe you want to live-tweet your spiral in real-time. Either way, multiple screens are a pro move.

- **Noise-Cancelling Headphones:** Block out the world while you doom scroll. You don't need distractions like loved ones telling you to "take a break" or "go outside." Focus is everything, and with noise-cancelling headphones, it's just you, your phone, and the end of the world.

The Professional Doom Scroller's Routine

Like any professional, you need a routine that keeps you at peak performance. Doom scrolling without structure can lead to burnout—or worse, real-life responsibilities creeping in. Here's a sample routine that will help you maintain maximum doom with minimum effort.

Morning: The Dread Kickoff

- **Start the Day with a Panic Check:** Before your feet even hit the floor, grab your phone and check the headlines. Bonus points if you're reading about the next global disaster before you've even brushed your teeth. This sets the tone for the day and reminds you that, no matter how well things might seem to be going, we're all still on the edge of the abyss.

- **Scroll During Breakfast:** Fuel your doom with carbs. As you munch on toast, dive into the day's hottest doom topics. Aim for a healthy mix of economic collapse, climate change, and at least one celebrity scandal.

Midday: The Lunchtime Spiral

- **Check the Global Status:** Is society still functioning? Probably not. Lunchtime is the perfect opportunity to dig deeper into ongoing crises—what's happening with the stock market? How's the ozone layer doing today? Keep your doom knowledge up-to-date.

- **Snack and Scroll:** Opt for something crunchy —it pairs well with the crushing weight of the latest economic forecasts.

Evening: The Prime Time Doom Dive

- **Post-Dinner Panic:** Now that the day is winding down, it's time for the real doom dive. This is your moment to sink deep into the chaos. Settle into your scroll station, crank up your "End of the World" playlist (more on that later), and get to work. Whether it's a political scandal, a natural disaster, or the latest conspiracy theory, this is your time to binge the doom like it's your favorite Netflix show.

Crafting the Ultimate Doom Playlist

No doom scrolling session is complete without the perfect soundtrack. You need music that reflects the highs and lows of your digital despair—a mix of moody, melancholic tracks that keep you going when the headlines get rough. Here's a suggested playlist to accompany your doom journey.

The Official Doom Scroller Playlist:

1. **"The Sound of Silence" by Simon & Garfunkel**

Because nothing says "the world is ending" like this iconic, somber tune.

2. **"Mad World" by Tears for Fears**
A certified doom scroller classic. It's like this song was written for the moment you realize nothing makes sense anymore.

3. **"Everybody Knows" by Leonard Cohen**
Every Cohen song sounds like the soundtrack to the apocalypse, but this one is particularly fitting for when you're reading about government conspiracies and corporate corruption.

4. **"Breathe Me" by Sia**
Perfect for that moment when you're five articles deep into climate change disasters and you just need to feel all the emotions at once.

5. **"Space Oddity" by David Bowie**
For when you're contemplating escaping this planet entirely and wondering if Elon Musk's Mars colony is taking applications yet.

6. **"Gimme Shelter" by The Rolling Stones**
A great track for when you're scrolling through Twitter and a new catastrophe

seems to drop every five minutes.

7. **"No Surprises" by Radiohead**
   The soothing melody of this song will help you reflect on the gentle absurdity of a world that constantly surprises you with fresh disasters.

Pro Tip:

- **Create multiple playlists.** You'll want different vibes for different types of doom. For celebrity drama, go with upbeat indie pop; for global crises, maybe stick with the heavier stuff. The right music can elevate your doom scrolling from a passive hobby to an immersive experience.

Maximizing Your Doom Intake: Multitasking Like a Pro

A true professional doom scroller knows how to multitask. Why read one doom-filled article when you can be doom scrolling across multiple platforms at once? With a little practice, you'll be doom-multitasking like a pro in no time.

How to Master Doom Multitasking:

- **Tabs, Tabs, Tabs:** Open multiple browser tabs,

each dedicated to a different brand of despair. One for breaking news, one for Twitter hot takes, one for Reddit conspiracy threads. Cycle between them to keep the doom fresh.

- **The News-Twitter Combo:** While reading a particularly heavy article about economic collapse, keep Twitter open on the side to catch the latest celebrity meltdown. This way, you can enjoy a lighter palate cleanser between each major catastrophe.

- **Doomscroll + Snack Attack:** Make sure you've got snacks within arm's reach—no need to interrupt the flow of doom with unnecessary trips to the kitchen. Pro tip: salty snacks pair well with political scandals, while sweets are better for environmental disaster spirals.

The Power of "Just One More"

Every doom scroller has experienced the seductive power of "just one more." You tell yourself you'll read one last article, and before you know it, you're four hours deep into the latest news cycle. This is the professional's greatest tool—and their biggest downfall.

Mastering the "Just One More" Technique:

- **Set Small Goals:** Promise yourself that you'll

stop after reading *just* one more article. Then set a new goal after that one. It's like tricking your brain into believing you have control when, in fact, you've fully embraced the doom scroll life.

- **Track the Time (But Ignore It):** Keeping an eye on the clock adds a layer of tension to your doom scrolling session. "I'll stop at 11 p.m.," you say. "I'll definitely stop at midnight," you lie.

- **Embrace the Spiral:** The key to professional doom scrolling is knowing that there is no end. You're not scrolling to *finish*—you're scrolling because doom never sleeps. The sooner you accept this, the sooner you'll unlock the next level of doom mastery.

Conclusion: Doom Scroll Like a Pro

Becoming a professional doom scroller takes dedication, focus, and a finely tuned balance between panic and productivity. With the right setup, a curated playlist, and multitasking skills, you can take your doom scrolling to new heights. But remember: doom scrolling is a marathon, not a sprint. Pace yourself. You don't want to burn out before the next major crisis drops.

In the next chapter, we'll explore Existential Ennui: Embracing the Void, where we'll delve into the philosophy behind doom scrolling and why we're all so deeply addicted to watching the world unravel from the comfort of our screens.

CHAPTER 8: EXISTENTIAL ENNUI: EMBRACING THE VOID

By now, you're no stranger to the deep, dark, swirling abyss that is doom scrolling. You've absorbed enough bad news to make even the most hardened pessimist wince, and yet, you continue to scroll. Why? Why do we do this to ourselves? What is it about diving headfirst into the infinite void of bad news, existential dread, and social media despair that keeps us coming back for more?

In this chapter, we're going to explore the philosophy behind doom scrolling and why we're so deeply, *inevitably* addicted to watching the world unravel. Spoiler: it's not just because we love a good train wreck (though, let's face it, we do). There's something deeper at play—something that taps into the very essence of human nature, existentialism, and our search for meaning in a world that sometimes feels meaningless.

Welcome to the void.

Why Do We Doom Scroll? The Psychology of Despair

Let's start with the big question: **why** do we doom scroll? On the surface, it seems counterproductive. Why would anyone willingly consume bad news on a regular basis, knowing it'll only lead to more stress, anxiety, and the inevitable feeling that everything is spiraling out of control?

The answer lies deep within our brains—specifically, in our need for control. Here's the paradox: doom scrolling makes us feel informed and in control, even as it slowly erodes our sense of well-being. It's the same reason people watch horror movies—they want to experience fear, but in a controlled, safe environment.

The Doom Scroller's Dilemma:

- **The Illusion of Control:** We doom scroll because it gives us the illusion that by knowing what's happening, we can somehow control it. If you know all the latest news, then surely you'll be more prepared when the next disaster hits, right? (Spoiler: probably not, but we tell ourselves this anyway.)

- **The Need for Certainty:** Uncertainty is scary, so we seek out information—even if it's bad—because it feels better than not knowing. It's why you keep refreshing Twitter, hoping for some update that will make things feel *less* chaotic. Spoiler: that update never comes.

- **Negativity Bias:** Humans are naturally wired to focus on negative news. It's a survival mechanism left over from the days when our ancestors had to be hyper-vigilant about, say, saber-toothed tigers. Today, that instinct has evolved into refreshing our news feed every 10 minutes to check for the latest catastrophe.

We doom scroll because, in a strange way, it comforts us. It reassures us that we're not missing out on anything important. We're in the know. We're on top of things. And even though it's driving us slowly mad, it feels better than the alternative—being uninformed and, worse, *unprepared.*

The Void Beckons: The Philosophy of Doom

Doom scrolling isn't just a bad habit—it's a reflection of something much deeper. At its core, doom scrolling is an existential practice. We scroll because we're trying to make sense of a world that often feels chaotic, unpredictable, and absurd. If existentialist philosophers like Sartre or Camus were alive today, they'd probably be doom scrolling too.

The Absurdity of Doom:

- **Camus and the Absurd:** In his famous work *The Myth of Sisyphus*, Albert Camus wrote about the absurdity of human existence. Life, he argued, is inherently meaningless, and the search for meaning is a futile endeavor. And yet, despite this, we continue to search for meaning anyway. Doom scrolling is our modern-day Sisyphus moment—we're endlessly pushing the boulder of bad news up the hill, knowing full well it'll come crashing down again tomorrow.

- **Sartre and Bad Faith:** Jean-Paul Sartre wrote extensively about the concept of *bad faith*—the idea that we deceive ourselves to avoid confronting the uncomfortable truths of existence. In a way, doom scrolling is an act of bad faith. We tell ourselves we're staying informed, that we're doing something productive, but in reality, we're avoiding the bigger question: *what does all of this really mean?*

- **The Void as Comfort:** There's a strange comfort in embracing the void. Doom scrolling allows us to stare into the abyss without having to fully engage with it. We're passive observers of the chaos, insulated by our screens. It's existentialism for the digital age—acknowledging the futility of it all while simultaneously refreshing for the next headline.

How to Embrace the Void (Without Falling In):

- **Acknowledge the Absurd:** Accept that the world is chaotic and that your doom scrolling won't change that. But also accept that it's okay to keep scrolling, because sometimes, staring into the void is part of the process. Camus would be proud.

- **Laugh at the Absurd:** One of the key principles of existentialism is learning to laugh in the face of absurdity. The world is often ridiculous and tragic, but that doesn't mean we can't find humor in it. Memes are the perfect antidote to existential despair—so keep those cat memes coming.

- **Don't Seek Meaning Where There Is None:** Not every piece of bad news needs to be dissected for meaning. Some things just are. The universe is chaotic, and sometimes the best thing you can do is acknowledge that, shrug, and move on to the next article.

Doom Scrolling and the Search for Meaning

Despite the futility of it all, humans have an innate desire to find meaning—even in the chaos. Doom scrolling, at its core, is part of that search. We're constantly looking for patterns, for signs, for anything that might make sense of the world's madness.

The Quest for Patterns:

- **Conspiracy Theories:** One of the reasons conspiracy theories thrive in the doom scrolling environment is that they offer a sense of order. They provide a narrative—however wild—that explains the chaos. It's easier to believe that secret cabals are controlling everything than to accept that sometimes, things just happen without rhyme or reason.

- **Hyperconnectivity:** In a world where we're constantly connected to an endless stream of information, we're always seeking connections. We doom scroll not just for the news, but for the sense that everything is connected, that there's a larger narrative we're a part of. Spoiler: the narrative is chaos.

- **The Desire for Heroes and Villains:** In every doom-filled story, we instinctively look for heroes and villains. Whether it's politicians, corporations, or celebrities, we assign roles to the characters in our doom scroll saga. It's part of our search for meaning in a world that often feels devoid of it.

How to Cope with the Meaningless:

- **Create Your Own Meaning:** In the spirit of existentialism, accept that the world doesn't owe you meaning—you have to create it yourself. Whether it's through art, friendships, or finding the perfect balance between snacks and bad news, create your own small pockets of meaning in the chaos.

- **Find Joy in the Absurd:** If the universe is inherently absurd, then the key to survival is finding joy in that absurdity. Doom scrolling can be a grim hobby, but it can also be hilarious. After all, there's something strangely comforting about knowing that everyone else is just as confused as you are.

The Doom Scroll as Modern Meditation

Here's a wild thought: what if doom scrolling is our modern form of meditation? Stay with me here. Traditional meditation is all about being present, accepting the moment as it is, and not getting attached to thoughts or feelings. Doom scrolling, in its own twisted way, does something similar—it keeps us hyper-focused on the present, glued to the now, and reminds us that the world is constantly changing, whether we like it or not.

How Doom Scrolling Mimics Meditation:

- **The Present Moment:** When you're doom scrolling, you're deeply immersed in the moment. It's like time disappears, and all that exists is the endless stream of information flowing through your screen. You're present in the chaos, accepting it for what it is.

- **Mindfulness (Sort Of):** Okay, maybe doom scrolling isn't the healthiest form of mindfulness, but it *does* require intense focus.

You're hyper-aware of every breaking news update, every tweet, every twist in the unfolding drama. It's like a digital meditation—just, you know, without the inner peace.

- **Acceptance of What Is:** Doom scrolling forces you to accept the reality of the world, even when it's bleak. It's a form of radical acceptance, where you acknowledge the chaos without necessarily trying to change it. In a way, it's zen—if zen involved reading about natural disasters while eating chips at 2 a.m.

How to Doom Scroll Like a Zen Master:

- **Practice Non-Attachment:** Doom scrolling is like meditation in that it requires you to observe without getting too attached. Read the news, absorb the chaos, and then let it go. If you can scroll without spiraling, you've reached enlightenment.

- **Find Your Flow:** There's a flow state in doom scrolling, where you lose track of time and become one with the endless stream of information. Embrace that flow, but don't let it consume you. Zen scrolling is all about balance.

- **Detach from the Outcome:** In meditation, you're not supposed to be attached to any particular outcome. In doom scrolling, this means accepting that no matter how much you scroll, you won't fix the world's problems. Let go of the need to solve everything and just *be* with the chaos.

Staring into the Abyss (And Smiling)

Doom scrolling is, in its own way, an existential practice. It's our attempt to make sense of a chaotic world, to find meaning where there often is none, and to embrace the absurdity of it all. But the key to surviving the doom scroll isn't in avoiding the void—it's in embracing it.

By acknowledging the chaos, laughing at the absurdity, and finding your own sense of meaning, you can navigate the world of doom scrolling without losing yourself in it. And remember: even though the world may feel like it's unraveling, you're not alone. We're all scrolling together, staring into the same void.

In the next chapter, we'll explore Pretending to Stop Doom Scrolling (But Don't)—because, let's face it, you're not quitting anytime soon, but you can at least make people *think* you're taking a break.

CHAPTER 9: PRETENDING TO STOP DOOM SCROLLING (BUT DON'T)

At some point in your doom scrolling career, someone—whether it's a well-meaning friend, your therapist, or a random internet stranger—will suggest that maybe, just maybe, you should take a break. "Step away from the phone," they'll say, with a tone of genuine concern. "You need to unplug and detox." And, deep down, you'll know they're right.

But who are we kidding? You're not going to stop

doom scrolling. Not really. The world is in perpetual chaos, and you've got to stay *informed*, right? However, there's an art to making it *look* like you're taking a break while secretly continuing your doom-filled descent into the abyss. The goal isn't to quit—oh no—the goal is to give the *appearance* of balance. That way, you can maintain relationships, get people off your back, and still keep up with the latest catastrophe.

In this chapter, we'll cover the best ways to pretend you've stopped doom scrolling, while ensuring you don't miss a single apocalyptic headline.

Announce Your Break (Publicly, of Course)

Step one in pretending to stop doom scrolling is to make a grand public declaration. You need people to believe you've seen the error of your ways and are now pursuing a healthier, more balanced lifestyle. Naturally, the best way to do this is by posting about it on social media.

Crafting the Perfect Break Announcement:

- **Be Dramatic:** "I've decided to take a much-needed break from the digital world. It's time to reconnect with what truly matters: life, nature, and my own peace of mind."

- **Sound Reflective:** "After some deep reflection, I've realized that constantly consuming bad news isn't helping anyone. It's time for me to focus on positive energy and self-care."

- **Incorporate a Buzzword:** Mention detox, mindfulness, or wellness. Maybe even throw in a yoga emoji for good measure. "I'm taking a digital detox to reclaim my peace. See you in a week!"

- **Add a Timeframe:** Give yourself an arbitrary length of time for your "break." It could be a day, a week, or "until I feel ready to return." The key is to leave it open-ended so you can come back whenever you want—probably in less than 24 hours.

The public declaration serves two purposes: it gets people off your back (because you *are* "taking a break"), and it makes you look like a thoughtful, balanced human who's taking care of their mental health. Win-win.

Create the Illusion of Balance

Now that you've announced your "break," it's time to create the illusion of balance. This is where things get tricky—because while you want people to think you've quit doom scrolling cold turkey, you'll still need to sneak in a scroll or two (or twenty). The trick is to mix in other activities to make it *look* like you've found harmony in your life.

Ways to Appear Balanced:

- **Post Nature Pics:** Everyone knows that nature is the ultimate antidote to doom scrolling. Take a picture of a tree, a sunset, or a body of water (bonus points if you're holding a coffee in the shot), and caption it with something like, "Taking time to enjoy the simple things."

- **Share Your Healthy Habits:** Mention a yoga class you *may or may not have* attended, post a photo of a green smoothie (you can buy one just for the pic, no need to actually drink it), or talk about how you're reading *actual books* now instead of news articles. "Loving this new novel —it's nice to be off my phone and get lost in a story."

- **Fake a Hobby:** Even if you don't have time for hobbies (because doom scrolling is your hobby), it's important to at least pretend. Mention a new "project" you've started: "Trying my hand at painting—so relaxing to create without distractions! #Unplugged #ZenLife."

- **Post Rarely (But Not Never):** Instead

of ghosting social media completely, pop in occasionally with non-doom-related content. A random post about how much you love fall, a photo of your dog, or an update on your sourdough starter (because that's still a thing, right?). This creates the illusion that you're still "online," just not buried in doom.

Set Up "Discreet" Doom Scroll Sessions

While everyone else is under the impression that you're blissfully enjoying your digital detox, you'll need to find sneaky ways to continue doom scrolling without getting caught. This requires some stealth, but it's not impossible.

How to Doom Scroll in Secret:

- **Use Incognito Mode:** If you're worried about someone checking your browser history (or if your significant other has a tendency to glance over your shoulder), use incognito mode while scrolling through news sites. That way, there's no trace of your descent into the doom void.

- **Late-Night Scrolling:** The best time to doom scroll in secret is late at night, when everyone else is asleep. Dim the brightness on your phone, plug in your noise-canceling headphones, and dive into Twitter's darkest corners without anyone knowing.

- **Check News During "Bathroom Breaks"**: No one will question the length of your "bathroom break" if you emerge from it looking slightly refreshed (though maybe don't spend *too* long in there). It's the perfect time to catch up on the latest global crises without raising suspicion.

- **Use a Different Device**: If people expect you to be "off your phone," try using a different device to continue your doom scrolling. Maybe your tablet, laptop, or the old smartphone you have tucked in a drawer for emergencies (and by "emergencies," I mean doom scrolling emergencies).

Blame the Algorithm

When you inevitably slip up and someone catches you mid-scroll, it's important to have a solid excuse. Enter: the algorithm. It's the ultimate scapegoat for your inability to quit doom scrolling.

How to Blame the Algorithm:

- **Act Surprised**: "Oh wow, I wasn't even looking for bad news—this just popped up in my feed!

You know how these algorithms are, they just keep showing you things you don't even want to see."

- **Play the Victim:** "I swear, I was trying to take a break, but Twitter *keeps* sending me notifications! It's like they're trying to drag me back in. Honestly, it's the algorithm's fault, not mine."

- **Redirect the Blame:** "You know, these social media platforms are designed to keep us hooked. It's so hard to escape—have you seen the documentaries about this? It's terrifying."

By blaming the algorithm, you can deflect any personal responsibility and make it seem like you're just an innocent bystander in the battle between your brain and big tech.

Announce Your Return to Doom Scrolling

Eventually, you'll need to "officially" return from your break. This is a delicate moment—you don't want to make it look like you caved (even though you probably never really left), but you also need to ease back into the doom scroll with grace.

How to Craft Your Return:

- **Be Humble:** "I took a break, and it was *so* refreshing, but now I feel ready to return to the digital world with a more mindful approach." Translation: "I never really left, but I want you to think I'm a changed person."

- **Mention Your Growth:** "After some much-needed time away, I've realized how important it is to stay informed, but also to balance that with self-care." Translation: "I'll be doom scrolling in moderation now. Maybe."

- **Sneak in a Little Doom:** This is the perfect time to subtly share some of the doom you've been secretly consuming. "It's wild how much has happened while I was away. Did you hear about the latest with the environment? Crazy stuff."

The Cycle Repeats

Now that you've mastered the art of pretending to quit doom scrolling, you can repeat the cycle whenever you need a break from people telling you to "unplug." Announce your break, secretly keep scrolling, and then return triumphantly. No one needs to know that you never really stopped.

Pro Tip: Plan Breaks Strategically

- Take a "break" when there's a particularly chaotic news cycle—it'll make your return all the more impressive. "I stayed away from my phone during the whole political scandal? I didn't even know!"

- Space out your breaks, so you don't look too dependent on the doom. You want people to think you're in control of your scrolling habits, even if you're definitely not.

Conclusion: Never Stop (But Make It Look Like You Did)

Pretending to stop doom scrolling is an essential skill for any pro. It keeps your social life intact, gives you the appearance of balance, and allows you to keep consuming bad news in secret. With the right strategies, you can maintain the illusion of wellness while still staying up-to-date on the world's most terrifying headlines. It's all about balance (or the appearance of it, anyway).

In the next chapter, we'll explore The Future of Doom Scrolling, where we'll speculate about what doom scrolling might look like in a world of virtual reality, AI-driven newsfeeds, and increasingly apocalyptic vibes. Because one thing's for sure—doom scrolling isn't going anywhere.

isn't going anywhere.

CHAPTER 10: THE FUTURE OF DOOM SCROLLING

Welcome to the year 2044. You're sitting in your minimalist, tech-optimized living pod, scrolling through your virtual newsfeed. But you're not just using a phone or tablet anymore—oh no. You're doom scrolling directly through your neural implant. Headlines flash across your augmented reality glasses. You receive a push notification from your AI news curator, DoomBot3000, who's found fresh existential crises just for you. In a world that's more interconnected, automated, and chaotic than ever, doom scrolling has evolved into something… more.

In this chapter, we'll explore where doom scrolling is headed. As technology advances, so too does the way we consume our daily dose of despair. What does doom scrolling look like in a world where AI generates personalized newsfeeds, virtual reality blurs the line between reality and fiction, and algorithms can predict your every anxious thought before you even have it? Let's peek into the (potentially terrifying) future of doom scrolling.

Neural Implants and Direct Brain Scrolling

The future of doom scrolling is hands-free—literally. Gone are the days when you needed to reach for your phone or sit hunched over a laptop. In the near future, you'll have neural implants that allow you to scroll directly with your thoughts. Imagine reading the news without having to move a muscle! The headlines will simply stream across your vision, overlaying your real-world surroundings in a way that makes it nearly impossible to escape.

How It Works:

- **Brain-Integrated Newsfeeds:** With a neural implant, you'll receive news updates directly into your brain, like a subconscious news ticker you can't turn off. Want to know what's happening with the economy? Just think about it, and the latest article will pop up in your mind. No need to open a browser—you're already plugged in.

- **Thought-Controlled Scrolling:** Tired of swiping with your fingers? In the future, you'll be able to scroll through news stories just by thinking about it. Eye movement or brainwave patterns will control your doom feed. Blink twice to scroll down, raise an eyebrow to open a new article.

- **24/7 Headlines:** The downside (or upside, depending on how you see it) is that doom scrolling becomes an ever-present part of your life. Even while making breakfast, walking the dog, or sleeping, your neural implant can feed you a steady stream of headlines about the next global disaster.

Benefits:

- You'll never miss breaking news again. You'll literally be plugged into the world at all times.

- Multitasking becomes easier—now you can doom scroll and live your life *simultaneously*.

Downsides:

- There's no escape. How do you "take a break" from doom scrolling when it's happening in your brain? The future is bleak—*and* so is your mental space.

AI-Powered Doom Bots: Personalized Crisis Delivery

In the future, your news won't just be curated by algorithms—it will be generated by AI specifically designed to cater to your unique brand of anxiety. Enter the Doom Bot: your personal AI assistant, constantly scouring the web for the most relevant catastrophes and crafting stories just for you.

How AI Doom Bots Work:

- **Hyper-Personalization:** Doom Bots analyze your past scrolling habits, your search history, your emotional responses to news, and even your biometric data (heart rate, sweat levels, etc.) to deliver *exactly* the kind of doom you crave. Are you particularly interested in climate change disasters? Doom Bot will serve up the latest news about melting ice caps and rising sea levels—along with a few predictions about when your favorite coastal city will be underwater.

- **Predictive Anxiety:** Advanced AI will be able to predict what kind of doom you're most likely to worry about next. Are you anxious about global pandemics? Doom Bot will preemptively send you articles about the latest viral outbreak *before* you even know it's happening. Feeling like the economy's on the verge of collapse? Doom Bot has you covered with real-time updates on market crashes.

- **Emotionally Responsive News:** Doom Bots won't just give you any old news—they'll customize the tone and style of the articles to match your emotional state. Feeling calm? Doom Bot will ease you into a crisis with a gentle "You may want to sit down for this." Feeling stressed? Doom Bot might just hit you with "Hold onto your hat, the end is nigh."

Benefits:

- **Tailored Doom:** Every headline is crafted specifically to push your buttons. No more wasting time scrolling through boring, irrelevant news!

- **Maximum Efficiency:** Doom Bot will summarize the most important facts, so you can absorb more dread in less time.

Downsides:

- **Doom Overload:** Your anxiety levels might

skyrocket when Doom Bot predicts your worries before you've even had them.

- **Trust Issues:** Can you really trust an AI that's designed to *optimize* your despair?

Virtual Reality Doom Scrolling: Enter the Crisis Zone

Why scroll through news on a screen when you can **step inside** the crisis? The future of doom scrolling will blur the lines between reality and fiction through immersive **virtual reality (VR)**. Imagine donning your VR headset and being transported directly into the heart of the latest disaster zone. Why read about a wildfire when you can *feel* the heat?

How VR Doom Scrolling Works:

- **Immersive Crisis Experiences:** Instead of reading articles or watching videos, you'll be able to *live* the news. VR doom scrolling will place you directly in the action. Want to see the effects of rising sea levels? Put on your headset and wade through virtual floodwaters in your own neighborhood. Curious about the latest political unrest? Walk through the streets of a virtual protest, complete with angry mobs and riot police.

- **Interactive News:** In VR, you won't just observe the news—you'll be able to interact with it. Pick up objects, interview virtual characters, and explore the disaster in real time. It's like playing a video game, except the stakes are much, much higher (and scarier).

- **Doom in 360 Degrees:** VR doom scrolling will be a full sensory experience. You'll hear the sounds of hurricanes, feel the rumble of earthquakes, and watch the world crumble around you—all from the comfort of your living room.

Benefits:

- **Total Immersion:** Doom scrolling will never be boring again. You'll *feel* like you're in the middle of the action, making every headline hit harder.
- **New Perspectives:** By stepping into the shoes of people directly affected by disasters, you'll gain a deeper understanding of the crises you're scrolling through. It's news with empathy—if empathy comes with a side of panic.

Downsides:

- **Too Real:** VR doom scrolling might be a little *too* immersive. There's only so much virtual disaster one person can handle before they start questioning whether the world outside the headset is real.

- **Mental Health Warning:** The line between reality and virtual doom will blur, which could lead to some serious existential crises. Can you handle watching the world burn in 3D?

Augmented Reality News: Doom Delivered to Your Daily Life

While VR immerses you in a fully virtual world, **augmented reality (AR)** doom scrolling will bring the news to you—literally. Imagine walking down the street and seeing real-time headlines overlaid onto your surroundings, turning every moment of your life into a doom scroll session. It's like Pokémon Go, but instead of catching cute creatures, you're collecting apocalyptic updates.

How AR Doom Scrolling Works:

- **Overlaying Reality with News:** With AR glasses or contacts, you'll be able to see news headlines hovering over buildings, on street signs, or even floating in the air as you walk. For example, you might pass a park and see a headline that reads, "New Study Reveals Air Pollution Levels in Your Area Are Worse Than Expected!" Or while grocery shopping, you could get an alert: "Food Prices Expected to Skyrocket Due to Climate Crisis."

- **Interactive Headlines:** You'll be able to tap (or blink) on headlines to expand them, get real-time updates, and watch video footage without ever taking out your phone. Doom scrolling will be integrated into your everyday life, seamlessly blending the real world with the digital one.

- **Location-Based News:** AR doom scrolling will provide hyper-localized news. As you move through different neighborhoods or cities, the news you receive will change to reflect the specific crises happening in that area. For example, if you're near the coast, you'll get updates about rising sea levels; if you're downtown, you might get alerts about crime rates or political protests nearby.

Benefits:

- **Doom on the Go:** You'll never have to stop what you're doing to catch up on the latest disaster. The news will follow you wherever you go, integrated into your daily routine.

- **Hyper-Local Updates:** AR doom scrolling makes the news more personal and relevant to your life, ensuring you're always aware of what's happening around you.

Downsides:

- **No Escape:** With news literally hovering in your field of vision at all times, it's hard to find a moment of peace. Even a walk in the park becomes a reminder that the world is on fire.

- **Constant Distractions:** AR doom scrolling could make it hard to focus on anything else. How do you enjoy dinner with friends when the latest climate disaster is flashing across your table?

The Rise of Predictive Doom: AI Forecasters

The future of doom scrolling isn't just about reporting what's already happened—it's about predicting what's going to happen next. With advances in AI and data analysis, news platforms will be able to forecast future crises with unsettling accuracy. Why wait for a disaster to unfold when you can be anxious about it *before* it even happens?

How Predictive Doom Works:

- **AI-Generated Predictions:** Advanced AI algorithms will analyze vast amounts of data

—from climate patterns to social media trends —to predict the next big disaster. You'll get notifications like, "Doom Alert: 75% Chance of Economic Meltdown Next Quarter," or "Prepare for Panic: Scientists Predict Major Earthquake in Your Region Within 6 Months."

- **Doom Timelines:** AI will generate personalized doom timelines for you, outlining potential crises you should be aware of in the near future. You'll have your very own "Apocalypse Calendar," complete with forecasts of when and where the next disaster is most likely to strike.

- **Interactive Risk Maps:** Using predictive doom, you'll be able to explore interactive maps that show where future crises are expected to occur. Click on a region, and you'll see predicted droughts, political unrest, or economic collapse —along with a countdown to when they're most likely to happen.

Benefits:

- **Always Prepared:** You'll never be caught off guard by a crisis again. With predictive doom, you can plan ahead and even start panicking early.

- **Data-Driven Anxiety:** There's something

oddly comforting about having solid data to back up your doom scrolling habits. After all, it's not paranoia if AI says it's coming, right?

Downsides:

- **Doom FOMO:** With so many predictions coming in, you might find yourself constantly worried about what's *next* instead of focusing on what's happening now.

- **Too Much Information:** Predictive doom can be overwhelming. It's one thing to worry about current disasters, but now you'll be stressing over future ones, too.

Conclusion: The Doom Scroll of Tomorrow

As technology continues to advance, so too will the way we consume bad news. Neural implants, AI-generated forecasts, virtual reality disasters—these are just a few of the innovations that will transform doom scrolling into a fully immersive, hyper-personalized experience. But one thing's for sure: no matter how advanced the technology gets, the human desire to scroll through chaos will remain the same.

In the future, doom scrolling won't just be a passive

hobby—it'll be a fully integrated part of our lives. Whether you're scrolling through a neural feed, stepping inside a virtual crisis, or getting real-time doom updates overlaid onto your surroundings, one thing is certain: the future of doom scrolling is bleak… but also kind of exciting.

In the final chapter, we'll wrap things up with Doom Scrolling and You: Final Thoughts on Finding Balance, where we'll explore how to live in a world of constant doom without completely losing your mind.

CHAPTER 11: KEEPING YOUR BALANCE

Here we are, at the end of our journey through the art, science, and future of doom scrolling. By now, you're an expert—you've mastered the fine line between staying informed and plunging headfirst into an existential spiral. You've learned the ins and outs of scroll techniques, explored the depths of the comment section jungle, and even peeked into a future where doom scrolling is integrated into every corner of your life. But before we close the book (pun intended), it's time to ask the big question: how do we find balance in a world of constant doom?

While doom scrolling is here to stay, the key to not losing your mind is figuring out how to balance your digital despair with real-life moments of joy, humor, and, dare I say, optimism. This final chapter will explore how you can still embrace your inner doom scroller while maintaining a semblance of sanity—and maybe even a little hope.

Acknowledge the Doom, But Don't Let It Consume You

The first step to finding balance is simple: acknowledge that the world is a mess. We live in chaotic times, and trying to pretend that everything is fine isn't going to help anyone (least of all you). The key, though, is not to let the constant stream of bad news consume your every waking thought.

How to Acknowledge the Doom (Without Letting It Take Over):

- **Set Boundaries:** It's okay to be informed, but it's also okay to set limits on how much you consume. Instead of doom scrolling for hours on end, give yourself a time limit. Say, "I'm only going to read the news for 30 minutes," and then —here's the tricky part—actually *stop* after 30 minutes. Put the phone down and walk away.

- **Take Mental Breaks:** It's easy to get caught up in a cycle of doom, but you don't have to be in a constant state of panic. Step away from the headlines, go outside, watch a silly video, or engage in something that has absolutely nothing to do with the world's problems. Remember, doom scrolling is about *balance*.

- **Stay Present:** Doom scrolling often pulls us into the future—constantly worrying about what's coming next. Instead, try focusing on the present moment. What can you control *right now*? What's happening in your immediate surroundings that isn't a disaster? (There's always something, even if it's just your cat staring at a wall for no reason.)

Laugh at the Absurdity of It All

One of the best coping mechanisms for doom scrolling is humor. If you can't laugh at the absurdity of the world, you'll end up crying into your snack stash at 2 a.m. (not that there's anything wrong with that, of course). The truth is, the world *is* absurd. The more you embrace that, the easier it becomes to doom scroll without spiraling into a black hole of despair.

Ways to Laugh in the Face of Doom:

- **Follow Funny Accounts:** Make sure your

social media feed includes accounts that make you laugh. Balance the serious stuff with memes, ridiculous videos, and anything that brings some levity to your doom scroll session. The world might be falling apart, but that doesn't mean you can't enjoy a well-timed cat meme.

- **Find the Irony:** Sometimes, the news is so ridiculous that it becomes unintentionally hilarious. Let yourself find the humor in the contradictions, the over-the-top headlines, and the sheer absurdity of it all. If the end is nigh, at least go out laughing.

- **Share the Laughs:** If you find something funny in your doom scroll, share it with a friend. It helps break up the heaviness and reminds you that even in the darkest times, there's always room for a little humor.

Stay Connected to People (Not Just Screens)

Doom scrolling is often a solitary activity. You, your screen, and an endless stream of bad news. But humans are social creatures, and one of the best ways to counterbalance the doom is by connecting with real people—friends, family, or even strangers who aren't discussing the end of the world.

How to Reconnect (Without Ignoring the Doom):

- **Talk to People in Person:** Sounds simple, but it's easy to forget how good it feels to talk to someone face-to-face when you've been staring at your screen for hours. Meet up with a friend for coffee, have a real conversation (preferably not about how doomed we all are), and remind yourself that life still exists beyond the scroll.

- **Doom Scroll Together:** If you *must* doom scroll, do it with someone else. Share headlines, compare absurd conspiracy theories, and laugh about how ridiculous it all is. Misery loves company, and sometimes doom scrolling with a friend makes it feel less overwhelming.

- **Share Solutions, Not Just Problems:** It's easy to fall into the trap of only sharing bad news. But every once in a while, make an effort to share something positive or hopeful. Whether it's a small win for the environment, a good deed someone did, or a new scientific breakthrough, remind yourself—and others—that not everything is terrible all the time.

Curate Your Feed (Like a Pro)

One of the most effective ways to maintain your mental health while doom scrolling is to take control of what you're consuming. You don't have to read *every* headline or follow *every* apocalyptic account. Curate your doom scroll experience so that it's balanced, diverse, and not completely overwhelming.

How to Curate Your Doom Scroll:

- **Unfollow or Mute Accounts:** If certain accounts or news outlets are sending you into a spiral of despair, it's okay to unfollow them or mute them temporarily. You can always check back in later, but for now, protect your peace.

- **Add Positive News Sources:** Sprinkle in some accounts that focus on good news, positive change, and inspiring stories. Follow nature photographers, artists, or anything that gives you a break from the doom. Your feed should be a mix of reality and optimism.

- **Be Selective:** You don't need to know *everything* that's happening in the world. Focus on the topics that matter most to you and skip the rest. Overloading yourself with too much information can make the world feel more chaotic than it already is.

Embrace the Idea of "Good Enough"

There's a temptation with doom scrolling to think that if you keep reading, you'll eventually be able to *solve* the world's problems. If you just stay informed enough, read one more article, watch one more video, you'll figure out how to fix everything. But the truth is, you can't fix it all. And that's okay.

How to Accept "Good Enough":

- **You Can't Know It All:** The world is a complex, chaotic place, and no amount of doom scrolling will give you all the answers. You can stay informed, but you don't have to know *everything*. Accept that it's okay to be informed "enough" without obsessing over every detail.

- **You Can't Fix It All:** There are things you can control, and things you can't. Focus on what's within your power to change, and let go of the rest. You can't single-handedly stop climate change or fix the economy, but you can make small changes in your own life that matter. Start there.

- **It's Okay to Take a Break:** Even professional doom scrollers need to step away sometimes. You're allowed to unplug, breathe, and focus on something else for a while. The world will still be there when you return—doom scrolling isn't going anywhere.

Find Joy in the Little Things

While the world might feel like it's perpetually teetering on the edge of collapse, that doesn't mean there aren't moments of joy and beauty all around you. Sometimes, it's the little things that keep us grounded when the big things feel overwhelming.

How to Find Joy in the Chaos:

- **Look for Small Wins:** Not every headline is catastrophic. Celebrate the small victories—the cleanup of a polluted river, the passing of a law that protects wildlife, or even just the fact that you remembered to water your plants today. Small wins add up.

- **Practice Gratitude:** I know, I know—gratitude can feel a little cheesy, especially when the world is falling apart. But taking a moment to appreciate the good things in your life, however small, can help balance out the doom. Gratitude shifts your focus, even if only for a moment.

- **Embrace the Mundane:** There's something comforting in the everyday routines of life. Making your morning coffee, chatting with a neighbor, walking your dog—these little rituals remind you that not everything is chaos. Find peace in the mundane moments.

The Art of Balanced Doom Scrolling

At the end of the day, doom scrolling is an inevitable part of our digital lives. The world is a messy, unpredictable place, and staying informed is important. But it's also important to remember that while you can't control the chaos, you *can* control how you engage with it.

Doom scrolling doesn't have to consume you. By setting boundaries, finding humor in the absurd, curating your feed, and staying connected to the people and moments that matter, you can strike a balance between staying informed and staying sane.

So go ahead—scroll on. But don't forget to step away every once in a while. The world might be a disaster, but that doesn't mean your mind has to be.

And remember, whenever you need a break from the doom, there's always a cat meme waiting for you at the end of the scroll.

CHAPTER 12: THE WORLD'S MOST ELITE DOOM SCROLLERS

You've come a long way, dear reader. From casual scrolls to pro-level doom diving, you've mastered the art of absorbing bad news with grace, humor, and just the right amount of existential panic. But what if I told you... there's another level?

That's right. There exists a secretive world of **elite doom scrollers**—the best of the best—who use their skills not just to survive the relentless flood of world-ending news but to actively shape the course of global events. These aren't your average news junkies. No, these individuals work for governments, militaries, shadowy organizations, and secret societies, using their unparalleled doom scrolling abilities to predict, analyze, and even *control* the chaos that engulfs the world.

And here's the kicker: if you become truly exceptional at doom scrolling, you might just get an invitation to join their ranks.

The Global Doom Scrolling Elite: Who Are They?

The world's most elite doom scrollers are a carefully selected group of individuals whose skills go beyond regular internet browsing. These are the people who spend 18 hours a day scanning global news feeds, dissecting conspiracy theories, and interpreting every vague headline as a coded message from the Illuminati. They're plugged into secret networks, using classified technology to sift through vast oceans of data, spotting patterns that even the most advanced AI can't detect.

The Organizations Behind the Elite Doom Scrollers:

- **Government Agencies:** These doom scrollers work in the back rooms of intelligence agencies, tracking global crises in real-time. Think MI6, the CIA, and other acronyms that sound important. Their job is to predict the next political coup, environmental disaster, or global pandemic based on their finely tuned doom senses.

- **Military Think Tanks:** The world's most powerful militaries employ doom scrollers to monitor and analyze potential threats—from impending wars to alien invasions. These experts can tell you exactly when the stock market will crash or when a new cold war will heat up. They don't just predict the future—they help shape it.

- **Secret Societies:** Behind the velvet curtains of history's most exclusive secret societies (you know, the ones with creepy symbols), there are doom scrollers working in the shadows. They aren't just reading the news—they're orchestrating it. Some say the Freemasons have a secret task force of doom scrollers who control global events from behind the scenes. Others whisper about the Order of the Black Scroll, a clandestine group that communicates solely through cryptic memes.

- **Shadowy Corporations:** Think the tech giants don't know you're doom scrolling? Think again. Inside their secret underground bunkers (because of course they have those), elite corporate doom scrollers are feeding CEOs the latest data on global disasters to ensure they stay one step ahead. Ever wonder how certain companies always seem prepared for the next big crisis? Elite doom scrollers, my friend.

How Elite Doom Scrollers Operate

You might think you're a pretty good doom scroller —refreshing Twitter every 10 minutes, following every conspiracy theory thread, and tracking down obscure Reddit posts. But the elite operate on a whole different level. These are professionals, and they use technology, methods, and sheer willpower that would make even the most seasoned doom addict tremble.

Tools of the Trade:

- **Top-Secret Algorithms:** Elite doom scrollers don't just use Google. They have access to classified algorithms that comb through global news in real-time, sifting through the noise to find the real nuggets of doom. These algorithms can predict everything from political unrest to the next viral meme.

- **Crisis Simulations:** The elite use advanced simulation software to run every possible scenario of global collapse. Will it be a supervolcano, a rogue AI, or an angry billionaire with a grudge? They've seen it all—and they're prepared.

- **Dark Web Data Mining:** Forget the regular internet. Elite doom scrollers dive deep into the dark web, where the *real* conspiracies live. From secret government documents to anonymous whistleblower reports, they gather intel from the darkest corners of the web.

- **Encrypted Meme Communication:** Elite doom scrollers don't just read headlines—they communicate through memes. But not just any memes—these are carefully crafted, encrypted messages hidden within jokes and images. If you can decode them, you'll gain access to some of the world's most classified information (or, you know, the best cat videos).

Secret Initiations: How Do You Join?

So, how do you get into this elite group of doom scrollers? You don't apply for a job. No, no. That's not how this works. If you've truly mastered the art of doom scrolling, they'll find *you*. The initiation process is shrouded in mystery, but rumors suggest that if you reach a certain level of doom expertise, strange things start to happen.

Signs You're Being Recruited:

- **You Receive Cryptic Messages:** One day, while scrolling through your news feed, you might notice a strange message. It could be hidden in a tweet, embedded in a meme, or even encoded in a news article. If you're sharp enough to decode it, you'll know it's a message from the elite.

- **Your Algorithm Changes:** Suddenly, your news feed seems eerily personalized. It's like the headlines are speaking directly to you. No matter how niche your interests are, you're receiving exactly the kind of doom you've been craving. That's when you know you're being watched.

- **A Strange Package Arrives:** Some say that when you're close to being recruited, you'll receive a package with no return address. Inside, there's only a black notebook and a single instruction: "Keep scrolling."

The Invitation:

Once you've proven yourself worthy, you'll receive a formal invitation. Maybe it'll arrive in your inbox, or perhaps a shadowy figure will approach you on the street. However it happens, the invitation will come with a single promise: "Join us, and you'll never doom scroll alone again."

Perks of Being an Elite Doom Scroller

What's in it for you if you join the ranks of the world's most elite doom scrollers? Aside from the obvious cool factor, there are plenty of perks that come with the territory.

Perks of the Job:

- **Access to Insider Information:** Forget the regular news cycle. As an elite doom scroller, you'll have access to the real stories—the ones the public doesn't know about. You'll get breaking news *before* it breaks.

- **Invitation-Only Doom Scroll Events:** Ever wanted to attend a secret doom scrolling conference? Now you can. Elite doom scrollers meet in underground bunkers (or fancy rooftop bars, depending on the vibe) to share the latest intel and swap conspiracy theories.

- **Top-Secret Memes:** Regular memes are for amateurs. As an elite doom scroller, you'll gain access to the best memes on the planet—hidden, encrypted, and designed to blow your mind.

- **Unlimited Data Plans:** Naturally, you'll need an unlimited data plan for all your doom scrolling needs, and the organization's got you covered. Doom waits for no Wi-Fi.

The Dark Side of Elite Doom Scrolling

Of course, joining the ranks of the elite isn't all fun and games. There's a dark side to being one of the world's most powerful doom scrollers. The pressure is intense, the stakes are high, and not everyone makes it out unscathed.

The Risks:

- **Doom Overload:** Elite doom scrollers are constantly plugged into the darkest corners of the internet, absorbing crisis after crisis. It's not uncommon for them to experience **Doom Fatigue Syndrome**—a condition where even the most catastrophic headlines no longer evoke any emotional response. If you find yourself scrolling through an alien invasion headline and yawning, you might be in trouble.

- **Paranoia:** Spending all your time tracking global conspiracies can lead to, well, *believing* in global conspiracies. The line between fact and fiction can blur, and soon you're wondering if your neighbor's garden gnome is a spy for a secret government organization.

- **No Escape:** Once you're an elite doom scroller, there's no going back. The knowledge you've gained is too powerful. You'll always be plugged in, always aware of the next big disaster, and always one step away from total burnout.

Will You Be Next?

So, dear reader, as you continue your journey through the world of doom scrolling, keep an eye out for the signs. Maybe, just maybe, you'll get that mysterious message. Maybe one day, you'll decode an encrypted meme and unlock the door to the world's most elite doom scrolling society. And when that day comes, you'll know you've truly made it. But until then, keep scrolling, stay informed, and remember: the world is always one headline away from total chaos—and you, my friend, are always one scroll away from greatness.

CHAPTER 13: CONCLUSION

You've scrolled through the pages of this book with the same dedication and intensity you bring to your doom scrolling habit. Along the way, you've learned how to transform your anxiety-fueled hobby into a serious professional pursuit. You've mastered the techniques, created the perfect doom station, and even explored the secret world of elite doom scrollers who operate in the shadows.

But most importantly, you've learned that doom scrolling—despite its chaotic, overwhelming nature—can be managed with a bit of humor, some self-awareness, and maybe a few snacks along the way.

So, What Now?

If you've made it this far, congratulations. You are no longer just a casual doom scroller—you're a **serious professional**. You've turned what some might consider an unhealthy habit into an art form. Whether you're refreshing your newsfeed in the middle of the night or casually dissecting the latest conspiracy theory, you're doing it with purpose, skill, and maybe even a little flair.

Now, your journey as a professional doom scroller doesn't stop here. The headlines will keep coming, the news cycle will never end, and there will always be a new catastrophe on the horizon. But that's okay—because you're ready. You've got the tools, the knowledge, and the mindset to not just survive the chaos but thrive in it.

How to Keep the Balance

Remember, being a professional doom scroller isn't just about constant anxiety. It's about finding balance, managing your screen time (or pretending to), and knowing when to laugh at the absurdity of it all. The world might be full of doom, but that doesn't mean you have to be overwhelmed by it. In fact, some of the best doom scrollers are those who know when to step away, take a breath, and then dive back in— refreshed and ready to decode the next wave of bad news.

Will You Be Invited Into the Elite?

Who knows? Maybe one day you'll receive that mysterious message from the world's elite doom scrollers, inviting you to join their ranks. Maybe you'll even find yourself working behind the scenes for a shadowy organization that uses your doom scrolling powers for good (or, you know, questionable purposes). Until then, keep honing your skills, refining your craft, and never forget the golden rule of doom scrolling: there's always something worse around the corner.

Keep Scrolling, But With Style

As you continue your journey, remember to doom scroll with intention. Whether you're tracking the latest global catastrophe or diving deep into the bizarre world of comment sections, do it like a pro. You've got this. After all, you're not just any doom scroller—you're a serious professional now.

So, keep refreshing, stay informed, and most importantly, enjoy the ride. The world might be a mess, but at least you're prepared to scroll through it with expert-level skill.

Thanks for joining us on this journey through the wild world of professional doom scrolling. We'll see you out there—probably at 3 a.m., refreshing the news feed like the rest of us.

Until then: scroll wisely, refresh often, and don't forget to laugh.